THE RENAISSANCE

THE INVENTION OF PERSPECTIVE

CONTENTS

To Raphaël

It is true that art serves no purpose. That it makes no sense to go to museums. That books are boring and expensive and music pointless. That it is enough to eat and drink—although enjoying fine things is unnecessary—and sleep. What's the use of seeing a good film? Of laughing with friends? There is no use if it's not essential to life.

Carlo Caritani, Bello Monte, June 1957

Painting on cover: Andrea Mantegna,
Fresco on the Vault of the Marital Chamber, 1474.

Graphic design: Sandra Brys

First published in the United States in 1995
by Chelsea House Publishers.

© 1994 by Casterman, Tournai

First Printing

1 3 5 7 9 8 6 4 2

ISBN 0–7910–2824–0

ART FOR CHILDREN

THE
RENAISSANCE

THE INVENTION OF PERSPECTIVE

Among the natural wonders, the first and rarest is that I was born in this century when the Earth was explored, while the Ancients knew barely more than a third of it. . . . Knowledge has expanded. What could be more wonderful than . . . the invention of the printing press, conceived by the minds of men, created with their hands, and able to rival divine miracles? What's left for us but to take possession of the skies?

Gerolamo Cardano (1501–1576)
from his autobiography written in 1575–1576

By Lillo Canta

Translated by Carol Volk

CHELSEA HOUSE PUBLISHERS
NEW YORK • PHILADELPHIA

HOW A BOY NAMED RAPHAEL
MET THE PAINTER RAPHAEL

Raphaël loved paintings—especially old paintings. This passion began on his fifth birthday, when he discovered that he had been named after a famous Italian artist, born over 500 years ago, named Raphaël Sanzio. His parents, who loved Raphaël Sanzio's art, had even reproduced one of his drawings of a cherub on the cards that announced the birth of their son.

Just before he turned nine, Raphaël found a book that contained reproductions of the artist's paintings and was fascinated by the beautiful colors and people. Young Raphaël was solely interested in his namesake, despite his parents' attempts to interest him in some of the other talented artists who painted during the 14th, 15th, and 16th centuries—three of the most extraordinary centuries in human history that form a period known as the Renaissance.

Raphaël

As he got older, however, Raphaël became more and more interested in this marvelous period. He began to dream of becoming an artist one day. But he did not want to be just any artist, he wanted to be a painter, a sculptor, an architect, *and* an engineer, in the tradition of the geniuses whose work he so admired. With his pencils, he drew unusual bridges, bright houses with lots of hiding places, dishwashers with televisions screens, and many other strange inventions.

Despite his great admiration for Piero Della Francesca, Botticelli, Michelangelo, and Leonardo da Vinci, Raphaël remained particularly attached to Raphaël Sanzio, whose talent—and first name—he appreciated.

At first his mother was pleased to see her son so curious, but as his interest continued to grow, she became alarmed. For holidays and birthdays, he only asked for postcards of paintings or books on his favorite subject as gifts. One day his father brought him an electronic game, hoping to distract him from his obsession, but Raphaël was disappointed with it. Almost nothing could distract him from his passion—except soccer.

THE RENAISSANCE IS . . .

At about the age of 10, Raphaël began reading a great deal about the Renaissance. Sometimes he had trouble understanding the books and would ask his parents for explanations.

His parents tried to make their answers clear, each in his or her own way and with greater or lesser skill—it's not easy to explain a phrase like: "It was only in the 15th and 16th centuries that men believed themselves capable of making things as beautiful as those created by God."

Raphaël's father was a lecturer, professor, guide, writer, and expert on old paintings. He was very familiar with the Renaissance, which he often spoke on for adult audiences, but when faced with his son, he felt a little shy. Raphaël noticed his hesitation and found it funny.

"At the time of the Renaissance people were exploring the world and making exceptional discoveries," Raphaël's father told him. "Christopher Columbus landed in the Americas for the first time. Johann Gutenberg perfected the printing press, and soon the first books were published, allowing many more people to read the texts that had been influential throughout history. Nicolas Copernicus discovered that the Earth rotated around the Sun and was not, as people thought at the time, at the center of the universe, and Galileo proved that our planet was constantly turning on its own axis. In just a few years a genuine revolution in thought took place! The world started on the mad race that leads us to the present day.

Raphaël Sanzio
The School of Athens
1509–1510, detail.
Fresco, 25 feet 3 inches
wide at the base.

The painter imagines the
two greatest
philosophers of ancient
Greece, Plato and
Aristotle, engaging in an
intellectual conversation
within a huge
Renaissance church.

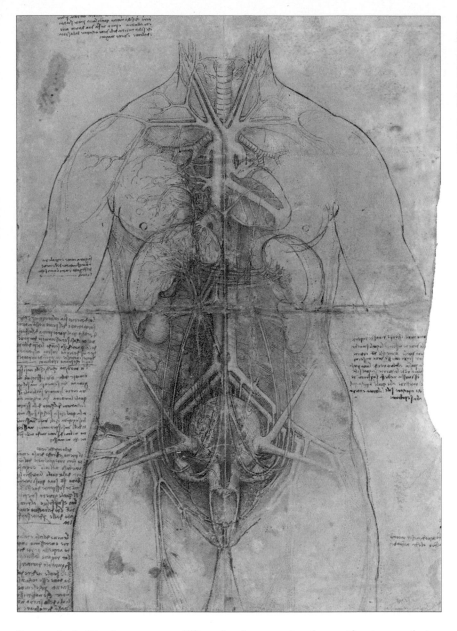

Leonardo da Vinci was
great Renaissance artist
His drawings describe
the natural world or the
human body, as in this
anatomical drawing of a
woman.
The painter-scholar
must have dissected
corpses to attain such
precision.

Leonardo da Vinci,
Anatomy Drawing. Pen
and wash on black stone,
circa 1510.

"People began to investigate and to understand humans and the planet on which they live. They explored the human body and created precise anatomical drawings of muscles, organs, and bones. 'Man is the model of the world,' wrote Leonardo da Vinci at the beginning of the 16th century.

"The Renaissance opened windows on the world through which people contemplated the magnificent and surprising landscape of the planet Earth.

"In order to know nature better, artists painted, drew, and described the vegetables and animals which form a part of it. Curiosity lovers emerged who collected rare stones and exotic vegetables, and artists became interested in these things as well.

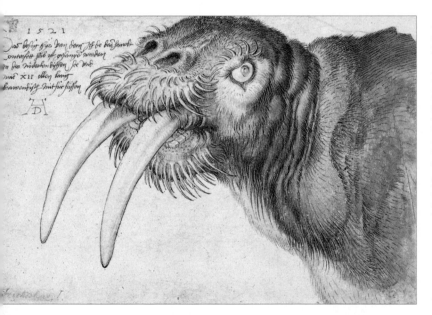

Albrecht Dürer, *Walrus Head*. Watercolor and pen on paper, 8 inches × 12 inches.

Dürer was a German artist who traveled to Italy and the Netherlands. He encountered many artists there and later wrote several theoretical works in which he outlined his ideas on art. Like Leonardo, Dürer explored the world through drawing.

"People also began organizing themselves in better and better ways, enacting many laws governing life in society and transforming their environment to tame wild nature.

"The city became more important. It was governed by a lord who decided on a policy of defense and growth, hopefully for the good of all. The lord often surrounded himself with artists, poets, and writers, who in some cases served as ministers or advisors. The Renaissance artist considered himself to be more an intellectual who *thinks* his art than a medieval-style craftsman or artisan who often merely shaped precious metals, sculpted marble, assembled pieces of wood, or painted with gold leaf without any larger purpose. During the Renaissance, the intention and meaning of the work became just as important as the skill of the artist. Da Vinci, for example, devised numerous inventions that had nothing to do with art, but which showed his interest in the larger world."

Andrea Mantegna, *The Family and Court of Ludovic III Gonzague.* Fresco in the marital chamber.

This painting dating from 1516 is the first known large-scale nude painted north of the Alps. The artist chose to represent Neptune (called Poseidon by the Greeks), the god of the sea, and his wife, Amphitrite, in a room whose columns are immersed in water. Renaissance artists were interested in the human body and often depicted it fully naked.

Raphaël listened without really realizing the impact these historical changes and scientific advances had on Renaissance art. He did not see any connection between these discoveries and the paintings he loved.

Nonetheless, without knowing why, he found this paternal prattle exciting with its occasional complicated words rising like bubbles in his head.

The Renaissance and the Ancient World

The scholars and artists of the 14th, 15th, and 16th centuries rediscovered the culture and thought of ancient Greece and Rome. That is why the period is referred to as the Renaissance (which means the rebirth), alluding to this new point of departure after centuries of slumber during the Middle Ages.

These days historians agree that the Middle Ages were not a period that was poor in creation and invention—one need only think of illuminated manuscripts or of Gothic and Romanesque cathedrals.

The Renaissance nonetheless marked a progressive change in modes of life and thought. Archeological digs and renewed interest in those vestiges of antiquity that were already known enabled people to become more familiar with the ancient Greeks and Romans. Ancient texts allowed them to discover the pursuits of Greek and Roman artists and philosophers. Learning from these studies, the people of the Renaissance made progress in science and art. Toward the middle of the 15th century, Pope Pius II visited the archeological sites of ancient Rome, Tivoli, and Ostia, and in 1462, he made a decree protecting the ruins by prohibiting use of materials taken from ancient palaces. Texts by Greek philosophers such as Plato and Aristotle, as well as other great thinkers of the Greek and Roman Empires, were sometimes translated into modern languages and analyzed by Renaissance intellectuals. They form an overview of the knowledge of the period.

Sandro Botticelli,
The Birth of Venus,
about 1482.
Oil on canvas, 5 feet 8 inches × 9 feet 2 inches.

This famous painting was commissioned by Giovanni di Pierfrancesco de Medici. The subject is taken from Greek and Roman literature, in particular from the Roman writer Ovid, whose *Metamorphoses* was extremely popular from the 14th to the 17th century. Botticelli represents the goddess Time covering Venus with a cloak. Venus is the Roman goddess of love and beauty, who according to Roman mythology, was born of the foam of the sea. On the left are the gods of the wind, including Zephyr, who transported the beauty to shore.

It is generally believed that the painter wished to depict the birth of humanity in this painting.

Giorgione, *The Three Philosophers*. **Oil on canvas, 4 feet 6 inches x 4 feet 9 inches.**

The subject of this painting has been interpreted in various ways. Some have seen it as three astronomers awaiting the appearance of a star. The characters could also symbolize three stages of human thought: the youngest being the Renaissance; the one wearing the turban, Arab philosophy; and the old bearded man, the Middle Ages. In any case, the painter depicts three characters observing nature. The youngest is taking geometrical measurements and the oldest has a manuscript whose open page is filled with geometrical forms and a compass.

THE MYSTERY OF THE AMBASSADORS

Raphaël's father, who was beginning to feel really awkward, decided to stop lecturing and to present his son with a difficult puzzle instead.

In order to find out if Raphaël could respond to a challenge without getting discouraged, his father confronted him with a problem which has left people gnashing their teeth for close to three centuries: the mystery of the ambassadors.

He showed Raphaël a color reproduction of a strange painting of two imposing, wealthy-looking figures. Among the objects surrounding them was a strange form at the bottom of the painting, in the center.

"Who made this painting on wood of these ambassadors? And what does this shape in the front represent?" his father asked, adding nonchalantly, "If you figure that out, I'll be very impressed, believe me. Keep the postcard—you'll need it."

Raphaël loved mysteries, but he realized by his father's tone that this one was not going to be easy. Confident nonetheless, he began looking through his books on the Italian Renaissance, although he was sure that he had never seen this painting before. As expected, he did not find the strange work. After depleting his resources, he stared at the painting for a long time, noting the sumptuous dress of the characters, the gold medallion worn by the man on the left, the presence of books, and the lute lying on the lower portion of the table next to a globe of the Earth. On the upper portion, covered

with a thick tapestry, the artist had painted a celestial globe and various scientific instruments of measurement. Were these two men famous scholars of geography at the time?

On the tile floor with its geometric forms sat a curious object that looked like a flattened football! Raphaël laughed at the idea—if this painting was done during the Renaissance, the shape could not possibly be a football. It was not flat, although it looked like it was, because it cast a rounded shadow.

The Ambassadors, **1533. Wood, 6 feet 10 inches × 6 feet 10 inches.**

"I'll begin by trying to find the artist," Raphaël said to himself, "then I'll see what to do. There's no trace of him in these books and no visible signature either. But look! There are inscriptions on the spine of the book on which the character on the right is leaning: *Aetatis suae. 25.* That's it—I've got my first clue. This must be Latin. I read once that educated people at the time read and wrote in Latin."

Raphaël painstakingly scrutinized the rest of the work with a magnifying glass and discovered the same type of inscription on the fur of a cuff: *Aetatis suae. 29.*

"No problem!" Raphaël said to himself. "I'll call my neighbor. He loves Latin, and he'll give me the translation pronto."

Indeed, two minutes later, without an instant of hesitation, the charming, elderly neighbor gave him the answer: " 'At the age of,' my young friend, that means 'at the age of.' "

Raphaël grew even more excited—he was sure he was on the right track to solve this mystery!

The Ambassadors, detail.

There was also a trace of writing on the bottom left of the painting, on a part of the pavement that was cast in shadow, but Raphaël was unable to decipher it.

"Shoot!" he cried. "Latin was used just about everywhere in Europe, so I still don't know the artist or what country the two men are from. I only know that the one on the left is 29 years old and the other is 25."

Thanks to the presence of certain instruments used for astronomy and navigation in the painting, Raphaël was able to place the artist in the late 15th century. The dress and tapestry covering the table suggested a Nordic country, perhaps the Netherlands or Germany. Raphaël's father made no attempt to contradict these ideas when they were mentioned to him, and he added with a conspiratorial air that artists from those countries made a point of carefully painting even the smallest details.

Raphaël was convinced: the painter was not Italian, but rather Flemish or German! He decided to poke around in his parents' library and skim through the books dealing with the painting of these regions. He was certain that he would find something of use, but he gave up after a few minutes of work and joined his mother, who was reading in her room.

WHEN PERSPECTIVE WAS
INVENTED

He showed his mother the postcard with
the painting of the *Ambassadors* on it.
She pretended to know nothing about it.
Raphaël's father had obviously filled her
in on the game.

"Too bad!" Raphaël said to himself.

He leaned over the book his mother
was immersed in, a novel by Marguerite
Duras called *Summer Rain*. Peeking over
his mother's shoulder, he read a confus-
ing scene: a young boy wants to stop
going to school because "they teach him
things there that he doesn't know." Raphaël exclaimed to his mother that this
did not make sense, since the whole idea
of going to school is to learn new things.

"Yes," she replied, visibly skeptical of
his argument, "you're probably right."

Pondering his all-too-sensible com-
ment, she picked up a big art book that
is sitting on the floor, opened it, and
began to tell Raphaël about perspective,
a term he has often encountered in his
reading without understanding its precise
meaning. He listened to her carefully, for
he sensed that this word was covering up
something mysterious and magical, that
it was an important key to understanding
Renaissance art—and to solving the puzzle posed by his father.

Surrounded by total silence, his
mother shared her knowledge of the mat-
ter:

"In the 14th century," she began,
"sculptors, architects, and painters in-
vented perspective. Thanks to this geometrical system, they were able to
represent a portion of reality."

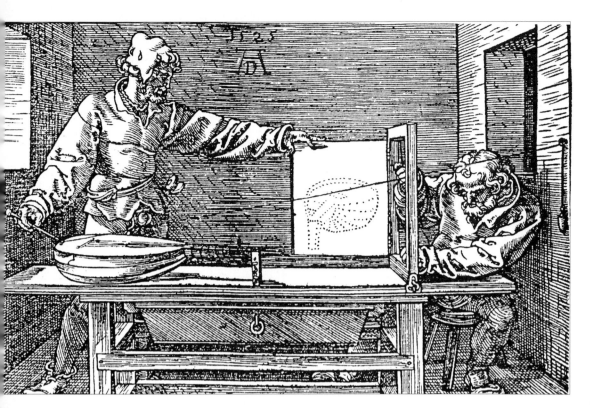

brecht Dürer, *Method
Drawing a Lute.*
graving on wood
cerpted from the
atise *Underweysung
r Messung*
structions on
asuring), book IV,
rnberg, 1525 and
38.

From the expression on Raphaël's face, his mother realized that this was not the right way to teach him—she was heading down the same fruitless path her husband had taken.

She started over:

"First let's take a few examples of perspective from everyday life. If you look at train tracks, they seems to be coming together, right? But fortunately, this is never really the case!"

Raphaël agreed, laughing.

"Here's another example. If a path is lined with trees, the two lines of trunks on either side seem to come together at the horizon and also seem smaller and less colorful the farther away they are."

"That's true," Raphaël agreed, after a moment's contemplation.

In 1525, the painter Albrecht Dürer wrote a book to teach artists how to represent even the most difficult shapes using perspective. To paint a lute, for example, Dürer advised the painter to choose a single point of view (marked by the ring fixed to the wall, to which a string is attached) and to project and outline the contours of the instrument with the help of a taught string (which represents the sight line) on a page that can be folded back on the frame.

"That is the type of visual experience that Renaissance painters reproduced in their paintings to give them the appearance of reality. Stand still in front of a landscape and close one eye, and you'll see a scene that looks very similar to those painted by the Renaissance artists. To represent a landscape on a flat piece of canvas or a sheet of drawing paper, you have to first imagine the point of view from which you are approaching this landscape. Then you arrange the trees on diagonals, meeting at a point (called the vanishing point) whose height will depend on how high you have decided to place yourself. If you are higher than this landscape, on a large bridge for example, the vanishing point will be very low. In that case you'll have a low horizon line and two thirds of the surface of your painting will be occupied by the sky. Often the horizon line is placed at the midpoint. The size of the trees, as well as the intensity of their color, will diminish the further away they are in the distance. The same is true if you add figures to the image.

 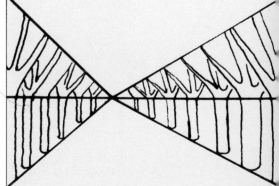

Architect, sculptor, and goldsmith Filippo Brunelleschi first demonstrated how to create the illusion of depth on a flat surface such as a sheet of paper, a canvas, or a wall.

The creator of the basilica Santa Maria del Fiore in Florence, Brunelleschi devised a small apparatus in about 1425 using a panel on which he had painted the church's baptistery. Opposite this painted panel he placed a mirror. Through a small hole in the door of the painted panel, one could see the reflection of the baptistery in the mirror.

Experiments such as this one helped Brunelleschi and another great Renaissance artist named Leon Battista Alberti (1404–1472) formalize and spread their ideas about perspective.

"Things that are small appear to be far away, while things that are large appear close. This variation in the size of things is called the law of proportions. You may notice that the color varies in a painting depending on the depth at which the painter places the characters and objects, and that they are smaller in the distance than in front. Imagine the sorts of problems a painter might have: if on the same piece of paper he was to draw a fly on the edge of the window right near him, and a big cow that he sees through the window 200 yards from his house, how big should each animal be? Which one will be larger?

"This sort of problem requires the kind of excellent knowledge of the laws of perspectives and proportions that the artists of the Renaissance had.

Perspective

Leonardo painted the episode of the three magi coming to pay homage to the newborn baby Jesus. The painter situates the vanishing point above the head of the Virgin Mary. The Virgin and the worshippers are within a triangle, which is itself inside a circular arch. All the characters seem to be moving about in disorder, while the trees and the two immobile figures bring calm to the composition. As always in the work of Leonardo da Vinci, movement and repose balance off each other.

This painting is unfinished.

Leonardo da Vinci, *The Adoration of the Magi,* 1481–1482. Wood, 8 feet 1 inch × 8 feet.

Before painting this work, Leonardo made several sketches and studies of it, including this one on pink paper. Here we see how he constructed perspective by means of the lines formed by the tiles and the architecture. The artist changed his composition when he painted the final version.

Leonardo da Vinci,
Perspective Study for the Adoration of the Magi,
1481–1482.
Pen and brown ink, silver lines and white touch ups on paper. 6.5 inches × 11.4 inches.

Alberti's Visual Pyramid

Alberti, a famous 15th-century architect, maintained that a painting should appear realistic and three-dimensional, resembling a view through a window. The frame of the painting should outline the view like the frame of a window, while all the sight lines should begin at the very edge of the painting and continue straight to one vanishing point with no alteration or shift in perspective. Alberti imagined a visual pyramid with a summit at the painter or viewer's eye and a base on the painter's work surface. This pyramid would be mirrored by the painting's apparent depth.

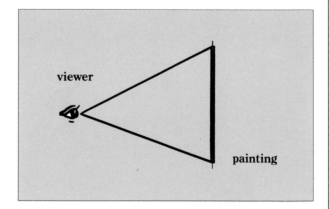

viewer

painting

Alberti's visual pyramid.

Renaissance thinkers considered a painting successful if it was orginal in its composition yet easily understood, balanced yet full of passion. A good painting tells a story in a captivating and clear manner.

Paolo Uccello, *Battle of San Romano,* around 1456. Wood, 6 feet x 10 feet 7 inches.

The painter Uccello was fascinated by the effects of perspective and used various points of view and many impressive foreshortening effects in this scene of the battle of San Romano, which took place between the Siennese and the victorious Florentines on June 1, 1432. Lorenzo de Medici, who commissioned this painting, kept it in his bedroom.

"Well before Brunelleschi's experiment and Alberti's writings, artists had approached perspective representation almost instinctively. In 1344, for instance, Ambrogio Lorenzetti painted *The Annunciation*. The top of this painting is flat and covered entirely in gold, but the tile floor simulates the space of the room, which is nine rows of tile deep. The bodies of the Angel Gabriel and the Virgin Mary have depth—an impression further accentuated by the folds of their clothing—and seem to occupy a large portion of the room, about four rows of tiles."

"The thin column at the center seems close to us, especially on the bottom. So the two figures must be between the column and the back wall," commented Raphaël.

Ambrogio Lorenzetti, *The Annunciation*, 1344. Wood, 4 feet × 3 feet 10 inches.

"That's right! The painter also uses the column to separate the two characters and to hide the vanishing point. Re-

In 1344, Lorenzetti depicted the Annunciation in a room with geometric tiles. The tiles allowed him to position the characters far to the back of the room. The slender column in the foreground supports the arches, which appear to be in the front of the room.

member what that is? Take the slanted lines of the tile floor and extend them until they meet. That is the vanishing point. Lorenzetti hid this point behind the central column here, do you see?"

But Raphaël had already thought of another question.

"Were the walls of houses painted in gold in the 14th century?"

"Rarely, but a gold background was often used by painters because it bestowed both real and symbolic value on the work. It gave it real value because real gold was used to paint these backgrounds or certain details of clothing, and gold was expensive. It gave symbolic value to the painting because the Virgin Mary and the angel were considered superior to men, and the use of gold places them outside the world of mere mortals. Painters later abandoned this practice."

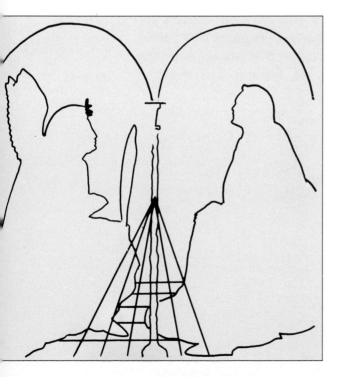

The Annunciation, or the passage of the Gospel in which the angel Gabriel announces to Mary that she will be the mother of Christ, is a very common theme in Western European painting. Many Renaissance paintings had religious themes.

Raphaël wondered if there was a connection between this gold background and the painting of *The Ambassadors*.

"No, there can't be any," he told himself. "The ambassadors are standing in front of a heavy tapestry."

"My painting is far more recent than Lorenzetti's, I'm sure," he said to his mother. "I think I understand perspective now. But who is this gentleman with the red hat and the gigantic hook nose?"

"It's the duke of Montefeltre," answered his mother, laughing. "He was a patron, which means he was an important, rich person who supported artists."

"But why show him from the side?"

"It does seem strange, but the duke had himself painted in profile because it was the trend in Italy at the time. Ancient Roman coins were imprinted with the heads of emperors in profile, which is probably why we find this particular angle in many 16th-century Italian paintings, event though it was very uncommon before then. Important people of that period sometimes compared themselves to the great figures of ancient Greece and Rome.

In this portrait, Piero Della Francesca combined an extremely close view—that of the bust of the Duke of Montefeltre, who seems near to us because of his size and position within the painting—with an infinite expanse of hazy landscape in the background. In the middle ground, between the bluish colors (also called cold colors) of the background and the foreground, the artist painted a wide river on which two sailboats are sailing.

Piero Della Francesca, *Diptych of the Dukes of Montefeltre, Portrait.* Wood, 1 foot 6 inches × 1 foot 1 inch.

"Let's get back to perspective," exclaimed Raphaël's mother, trying to recapture his attention. "Masaccio painted *The Trinity* on the walls of the Santa Maria Novella church in Florence. He constructed his work taking into account the position of the painting in relation to those who would see it in the church. By placing the vanishing point at the eye level of an observer, Masaccio created the illusion of a real, three-dimensional scene that is being observed from below. When hung, the painting looks as though it's a real recess in the wall, but the wall is actually totally flat."

"Who are the two people on the bottom?" asked Raphaël.

"The people who commissioned the painting and paid Masaccio for his work."

"How much did he earn for a painting like that?"

"We don't know in this case, but there are paintings for which we have that type of information."

Tommaso di Ser Giovanni, better known as Masaccio, painted this work on the walls of the Santa Maria Novella church in Florence in about 1425. It is generally considered to be the first use of systematic perspective in painting.

The artist situates the vanishing point at the eye level of the viewer, whom he imagines to be standing slightly below the painting.

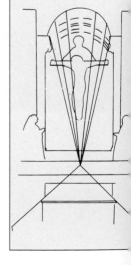

Masaccio, *The Holy Trinity with the Virgin and St. John,* 1425. Fresco, 21 feet 10 inches × 10 feet 1 inch.

e larger objects and
aracters are, the more
cise their contours
, and the brighter
eir colors are, the
ser they appear. The
aller they are and the
re they blend into the
ace surrounding them,
further away they
em to be. Gold
ckgrounds were
dually replaced by
dscapes in paintings
mmissioned by 14th-
ntury European
urts. The person who
mmissioned this
inting expressly asked
rnardino Pinturicchio
fill in any empty
aces with landscape.

Bernardino Pinturicchio,
*Saint Augustine and the
Child.* Part of the alter
piece of Santa Maria de
Fossi, 1495. Wood.

How were artists paid?

Some of the written contracts between clients and artists of the 15th century have been preserved to our day. Sometimes they are very official and have been notarized; sometimes they are simple notes, referred to in Italian as *ricordi* (memories), taken down by the person who commissioned the painting and by the artist.

This painting, finished in 1488, was the object of an official contract between the prior of the Ospedale degli Innocenti (Foundling Hospital) in Florence, Friar Bernardo, and the artist, Domenico Ghirlandaio.

The contracted signed by the two parties specifies:

—that the wood panel will be prepared (assembled, smoothed and coated) by the painter;
—that the painting will be painted entirely by Ghirlandaio and not by assistants (a common practice) according to the model already sketched on paper and approved by the prior of the hospital;
—that it will be painted with high-quality colors and that real gold powder will be applied as necessary;
—that the blue used in the painting must be ultramarine blue (an expensive paint made from a base of lapis lazuli powder imported from Asia, which was of excellent quality but was difficult to manipulate) at the price of four florins an ounce;

—and finally, that Domenico must finish the work within 30 months or be fined. He is to be paid 115 large florins, unless the prior considers that the work is worth less (the prior may have recourse to the advice of another painter in making this judgement).

Domenico Ghirlandaio, *The Adoration of the Magi*, 1488. Wood.

This painting, portraying a popular religious theme of the time, was the object of a very precise contract between the client and the painter. By the terms of the contract, the artist agreed to follow an earlier model drawn by him and approved by the client, to finish the work within the stated time period, and to use high quality paints.

As a talented artist, Botticelli was paid 78 florins and fifteen sous for this painting for the Santo Spirito chapel—a tidy sum, but one which also had to pay for the artist's expenses, including expensive gold powder.

These expenses were broken down in the contract to 2 florins for the ultramarine blue, 38 florins for the gold and the preparation of the panel, and 35 florins for his work (in the contract it is written "per suo pennello"—"for his brush").

Sandro Botticelli, *Virgin with Child between the two Saint Johns* (also called *Madone Bardi*), 1485. Wood, 6 feet 1 inch × 5 feet 11 inches.

"Look at the points of view chosen in these paintings," continued Raphaël's mother, "especially the ones by Andrea Mantegna, who loved surprising angles. It was a way of demonstrating his talents as an artist-geometrician and of arousing visitors' curiosity."

Andrea Mantegna, *Fresco on the Vault of the Marital Chamber,* 1474.

Height of the vault at its center: 22.92 feet.

Mantegna painted this fresco in the marital chamber of the palace of the Duke of Mantoue. He painted it with the expectation that it would be seen by a person standing at the exact center of the room, looking up at the ceiling. He manages to make us believe that a real hole exists in the ceiling.

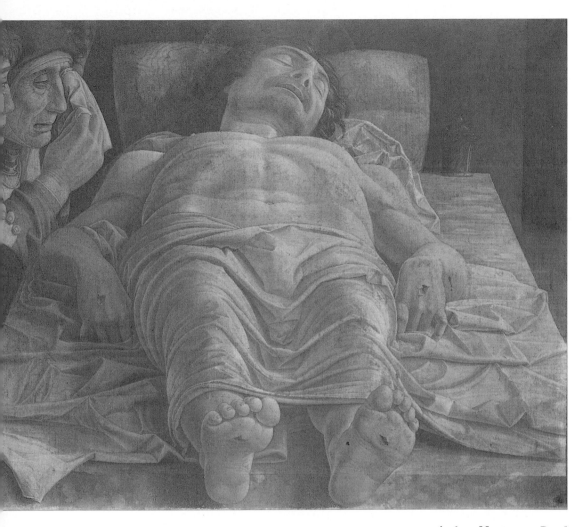

Andrea Mantegna, *Dead Christ*. Oil on canvas, 2 feet 3 inches × 2 feet 8 inches.

Mantegna creates the illusion in this painting that the viewer is very low, below Christ. The technique he uses here is called foreshortening. In this instance, the effect is quite striking!

"Are there paintings in which the painter mixes several different points of view?" asked Raphaël. "Where, say, one part is seen from above and another part from below or from the side?

He noticed that his mother was smiling the way his father did the other day.

"Yes, of course that exists. For instance there is *The Annunciation* by an anonymous 15th-century Flemish painter known as the Master of Flémalle. He used what is called instinctive perspective, as did his fellow Flemish painters in general. Using instinctive perspective means that the painter did not have formal training in perspective techniques but nontheless did arrange objects in his painting to convey depth.

"The result is an interesting twist on traditional perspective. In *The Annunciation* the Angel and the Virgin Mary are seen straight on and at the same time from above, and the same is true for the table. This is the first time a Flemish artist achieves such coherence in representation. What I mean is that in this painting the artist makes us believe in the existence of a room, with three walls that we are able to see. Where is the fourth wall?" she asked Raphaël.

Surprised by the question, he managed only to mutter, "What fourth wall?"

"The one that's missing, look!"

"That's right, it should be in front and hide the inside of the room."

"You're right! It's as if the painter had replaced it with a clear glass pane so that we could see inside."

"But why didn't this Flemish painter follow the ordinary rules of perspective? Didn't he know them?"

"He probably didn't know the theory, but he was perfectly capable of creating a painting using normal perspective. He chose not to do so because he wanted to place the emphasis on the objects on the table. The bouquet of white lilies and the book are important—they recall episodes of the New Testament from which the story of the Annunciation is taken. The lily signifies that the Virgin Mary is pure, white as a lily in a sense, and the open book signifies that with the birth of Christ, we are passing from the Old Testament to the New. For Flemish painters at the time, emphasizing these sorts of symbols was more important than respecting traditional perspective."

The Master of Flémalle, *The Annunciation.* Central panel of a triptych, 1427—1428. Wood, 1 foot 11 inches × 2 feet 1 inch.

hile Italian artists eated realistic erspective paintings, emish painters, hough able to recreate ality, did not respect e theoretical rules of erspective. The figures re, for example, are realistically large in spect to the size of the om. This is not due to ck of skill but to oice. The Master of émalle employs what ight be called "moral erspective," giving eater importance to e angel and the Virgin ary.

What was taught at school in the 14th and 15th centuries?

Young Florentines, sons of merchants or other middle-class families, were more likely to attend private or communal schools than the Catholic schools, which were somewhat neglected in Florence during this period. At primary school (*botteghuzza,* which can be translated as "small boutique"), children were taught to read and write, usually at the age of seven or eight but sometimes as young as four. Upon completing this first schooling, children were able to write simple business letters and use common legal formulas—the minimum skills necessary to manage a business or conclude sales and purchasing contracts. They then spent four more years attending secondary school (or *àbaco*), which was almost exclusively devoted to teaching mathematics. Some continued on to a university. At the time, it was believed that geometry and arithmetic sharpened children's minds; a Florentine banker named Giovanni Rucellai even said that arithmetic "makes the mind capable of understanding subtle things." Upon graduating from secondary school, these young boys were able to measure and evaluate the contents of containers and to calculate volumes and surfaces. Merchandise was transported in sacs or barrels of various sizes, so it was essential to be able to quickly and accurately evaluate their contents in order to estimate the value of the merchandise.

Florentine artists, having attended traditional secondary schools, were capable of quickly evaluating volumes and weights, a skill reflected in their paintings. The painter Piero Della Francesca even wrote a mathematical treatise (*trattato d'àbaco*).

The Florentines, educated as they were in mathematics and geometry, were very sensitive to games of perspective and proportion in paintings, which were similar to the daily exercises they completed in school as well as the daily challenges of their professions.

Piero Della Francesca,
The Flagellation of Christ,
around 1455. Wood, 1 foot
11 inches × 2 feet 8
inches, signed OPUS
PETRI DE BURGO
S(AN)C(T)I SEPULCR(I).

Here the painter
represents the flagellation
of Christ, an episode from
the Gospel. We do not
know for certain the
identities of the three
figures in the right
foreground, who may
simply be acquaintances
of the painter. The artist
places the figures of his
time, who seem to be
commenting upon the
historic scene, in the
foreground and the
episode of the flagellation,
which occurred more than
1400 years before, in the
rear of the composition.
The use of perspective in
this painting allows the
viewer to distinguish
between the different time
periods and makes the
events pictured easier to
understand.

RAPHAEL UNCOVERS AN
IMPORTANT CLUE

The days and weeks passed and Raphaël's interest in Renaissance painting seemed to fade. He went to school and played soccer with his friends—*The Ambassadors* seemed to be far from his thoughts.

His parents believed that he was cured of his obsession. His father was particularly pleased, for he feared that his son might choose to follow the same dead-end career path he did when he became an art expert: the small jobs writing for more or less prestigious journals, the low-paying jobs analyzing paintings for greedy collectors and gallery owners, the temporary teaching jobs, the lectures given to small audiences of exhausted people who have rushed in after work. His mother was less happy, for she believed that the choice of their studies and professions had its own rewards, despite their small income. She loved to spend evenings discussing old or modern painting or sculpture.

Unbeknownst to them, Raphaël continued to gather information. He was stubborn, and he was determined to find the solution to this enigma.

"What if Dad is hiding the books that would put me on the right track?" he thought one day. "That would be just like him."

So that Saturday afternoon, he slipped quietly into his parents' bedroom. A few novels were strewn about the floor and the night table, along with newspapers and art books. Three fairly large, slim volumes attracted his attention.

This small-scale painting depicts Saint Jerome reading in his studio. Antonello surrounded the saint, who has been credited with the translation of the Bible into Latin (the Vulgate), with his books, inkwell, and pen—as well as with the lion who is usually present in representations of the saint (he became the saint's faithful companion when the latter healed his wounded paw). The artist draws us into the painting in stages: first through the contours of the arch in the foreground, then by the lines of the pavement, which lead the eye to the back of the large room whose windows open out into an infinite landscape. He places the saint's studio in the middle of this vast interior space.

They were monographs from a series entitled "The Collected Painted Works of —." His father and mother had dozens of these and referred to them often. He picked up one devoted to Edgar Degas, a 19th-century painter, and put it down without opening it. He considered and rejected one devoted to Antonello da Messina, since the name was obviously Italian.

Antonello da Messina, *Saint Jerome in his Studio,* around 1474. Wood, 1 foot 6 inches × 1 foot 2 inches.

Hans Holbein, *Portrait George Gisze*, 1532. Distemper on wood, 3 feet × 2 feet 10 inches

But the mere sight of the cover of the third made Raphaël's heart beat faster: *The Collected Painted Works of Holbein the Younger*!

"Maybe he's the one who painted my painting," wondered Raphaël. "A German-sounding name would be just right."

He feverishly opened the book and began reading. He was so absorbed in the book that he did not hear the front door open.

His father suddenly entered the room and asked him to leave.

Raphaël could not pursue his investigation that evening, and the following

Friday, he discovered that the book had disappeared from the room. "I must be on the right track," he chuckled.

A few days later, he consulted the *Dictionary of Great Painters* and found: "Holbein, Hans the Younger, German painter (Augsbourg 1497/98—London 1543)."

"So he was a German painter. No wonder I couldn't find him in the books on the Italian Renaissance!"

The illustration opposite the article shows the portrait of a certain George Gisze, which the artist painted in 1532. The painting style was the same as *The Ambassadors,* with a tapestry covering the same table.

Upon reading the article, Raphaël learned that Holbein, born in Germany, lived in Basel, Switzerland, from 1516 to 1526, in London from 1526 to 1528, again in Basel, and finally, after a short stay in Antwerp, settled in London from 1532 to 1543, when he died of a plague that swept through London at the time. While in London, he painted portraits of well-to-do merchants and worked for the English monarchy. He painted *The Ambassadors* in 1533.

Raphaël was disappointed. There was nothing in the book about the identity of these two ambassadors or about the significance of the oblong shape in the front of the painting. He did have, however, the answer to his father's first question; for the second, he was going to have to find the book on the artist he had glimpsed a few days earlier. He wisely chose not to reveal his discoveries to his parents.

When he returned home, he joined his mother in her bedroom, hoping to discretely locate the book in question.

As he entered the room, he picked up and opened a fat book on the painter Masaccio, glancing at the table nonchalantly to look for the volume on Holbein the Younger.

"Holbein," he repeated to himself. "Hol-bein."

Raphaël liked the sound of the name. He had even tried to pronounce it as it would be in German: "Hool-baïn."

Only two of the three works from the "The Complete Painted Works" series remained. His father had taken away the one that almost certainly would have solved the mystery. He asked his mother a trivial question, but instead of answering, she eyed him with a slight smile and asked him what the subject of one of the Masaccio paintings was.

Raphaël had no reply, so she took the book and began:

"This fresco represents a religious scene where tribute money is being paid. Masaccio placed the vanishing point at the eye level of the characters and behind Christ's head at the center of the composition—using perspective to give value to the figure of Christ. Note that Saint Peter appears three times in this painting: on the left, in the center next to Christ, and on the right. Remember that perspective organizes a painting—thanks to perspective, the work looks real without actually being real. "The artist determines and sets the point of view and selects what objects or people are included. So even though they are based on real places, paintings are above all idealized sites where lines are pure and nothing unforeseen can happen. The sky is clear, and birds fly in formation, if that's what the painter wants."

Raphaël laughed at his mother's colorful description, but decided that nothing she was saying would help him with his mystery. He told his mother that he was going to bed and left.

asaccio, *The Tribute ney*, 1425. Fresco, 8 et 4 inches × 19 feet 7 ches.

Masaccio tells a story about Jesus Christ in three episodes, which he places across the canvas as if all three were occurring simultaneously. In the center, the tax collector (whose job was to collect a fee from people entering the city) asks Christ to pay the tax. Christ asks his disciple Peter, whom he designates with his finger, to get the money from the mouth of a fish, which we see on the left of the painting. On the right, Peter takes the money and gives it to the tax collector.

Fresco Painting

Fresco painting is a mural painting technique that was very popular during the Renaissance in Italy. The term *fresco* means fresh in Italian. When an artist paints a fresco, he uses water-based paint (as opposed to the oil-based paint often used on panels or canvases) and prepares the wall by coating it with several layers of plaster. A bit of sand or crushed marble is added to the final layer to ensure its smoothness and prevent it from cracking.

While this last layer of plaster is still damp, the artist applies the paint. The plaster must be damp when the paint is applied to the wall, so the painter must prepare only the surface area he thinks he can complete in one day. The plaster hardens as it dries, capturing the painting and fixing it durably to the wall.

If you looks closely at a fresco, you can sometimes detect traces of the different work days (*giornate* in Italian) that the artist planned. This gives scholars a sense of the time that was spent painting the details of what are often large compositions.

It took seven days to complete this sibyl's body, three for her clothing and one for each arm. Michelangelo was probably unhappy with the left foot painted by an assistant and went over the detail, which explains the small area covered by that day's work. Traces of nails on the face indicate that the artist used a model sketched in advance—the nails served to transfer the outline of the drawing onto the damp plaster, like the tracing of a drawing.

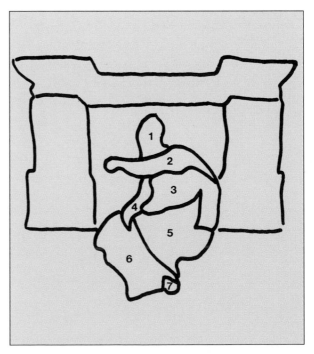

The Sistine Chapel

The Sistine Chapel is inside the Vatican Palace in Rome.

The chapel, which dates from about 1475, was completed during the pontificate of Pope Sixtus IV, hence the name "Sistine." The paintings on the chapel vault, which are still admired today, are the work of the great Renaissance artist Michelangelo.

The chapel's paintings include some 300 figures distributed over more than 1,000 square yards!

One can follow almost step by step the evolution of the enormous work, completed by Michelangelo and several assistants, by observing the traces of the work days still visible on the surface of the vault.

Michelangelo, *The Sibyl of Delphi*, 1509. Fresco.

This sibyl (in ancient Greek mythology, a woman who predicts the future), which is almost nine feet tall, is notable for its graceful form and its beauty. The breakdown into work days can be clearly distinguished.

THE SOLUTION TO THE
MYSTERY OF THE
AMBASSADORS

Raphaël made a decision: he would not sleep that night until he found the solution. He was tired of dreaming of the two ambassadors with their Germanic faces, which would glow in certain nightmares while the one on the left thrusted at the strange object with his finger. Why did this painting make him so uncomfortable when the painter was only showing off the wealth of the men?

He had read in the art dictionary that many of Holbein the Younger's engravings were about death and contained skeletons and other somber objects. It would make sense if, despite appearances, the subject of *The Ambassadors* is also serious and grave, so grave that Holbein hid it beneath a form—a formless form. Raphaël also had discovered in a German dictionary that *hohl* means "hollow, empty" and *Bein* means "bone." Hol-bein: Hollow-bone.

"Strange name," Raphaël mused.

By this point, he was a little upset with his father for giving him such a difficult and disturbing mystery to solve. That night, when the house grew totally silent, Raphaël got up and headed toward the library with the help of a flashlight. He closed the door to the room with its vast shelves of books and cast the light beam over the spines, arranged by category. He remembered one time when his father was angry at not having found a book he had been looking for at the library in town. He said then that "a badly-shelved book is a lost book!"

Raphaël realized that the best way to hide a book would be simply to shelve it in the wrong place. What could be safer than to hide a book among other books? He looked through the travel books, then the sociology books, then the rest of the books—all to no avail! He was on the wrong track again. He'd gotten lost in the labyrinth of his own ideas, and all because of these stupid ambassadors!

Then he thought of the kitchen.

"That's it," he whispered, "the cookbooks that mom keeps in the kitchen cupboard. What could be a better place? In any case, it's the only place left for me to search."

He slipped down the hallway, tiptoeing to the kitchen where the refrigerator was humming noisily. He banged it on the left side and the noise immediately stopped.

He opened the cupboard. The volume on Holbein the Younger was there, sitting straight up and to the right of a square book with a title that promised to reveal everything about the art of a successful veal roast. He took the precious work under his arm, returned promptly to his room, and turned on his desk lamp.

He quickly read the account of the painting, hurriedly ticking off secondary details, such as the presence of a signature he had been unable to decipher several days earlier on the postcard, "IONNES/HOLBEIN/PINGEBAT/1533," and the name of the two figures depicted: Jean de Dinteville, decorated with the order of Saint-Michel, and Georges de Selves, whose elbow is resting on the high table.

Then he discovered something about the painting that left him speechless—there was a human skull! He read the passage again. It said that the strange, unrecognizable shape at the bottom of the painting is a human skull! "Hol-bein," Hollow-bone! Now *there's* an original signature.

But Raphaël didn't understand how anyone could be so certain what the strange shape was. He read the sentence a third time: "In the center of the foreground, at the feet of the ambassadors, figures the anamorphosis of a skull."

That night, his sleep was riddled with visions of death. Skeletons bent over him and whispered terrible things in German, which, fortunately, he didn't understand.

The next day at breakfast, he rushed to his father and asked him right off, "What is the anamorphosis of a skull?"

A vexed expression flashed over his father's face, quickly replaced by a loud laugh. Against all expectation, his son had solved the mystery of the ambassadors.

"Well, all that's left for me to do now is explain it to you," he said.

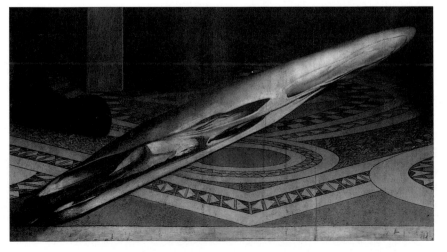

Hans Holbein the Younger, *The Ambassadors*, 1533. Detail from the bottom center.

"At the time the work was painted, the frame of the painting, which has since disappeared, must have been massively thick, extending a number of inches in front of the canvas itself. There must have been a minuscule hole in the side of this frame which would guide the viewer's eye along the right angle to clearly see the skull. An anamorphosis is a severe distortion in the perspective of an object. The two characters can be seen clearly by standing in front of the painting, but you have to look sideways from one edge of the painting to see the skull. Holbein combined two extreme points of view in the same space. You can see the results."

"But I don't understand," exclaimed Raphaël. "Renaissance artists tried to paint paintings that could be understood by everyone! Why is this one so hard?"

"Look at the dates. Holbein made this work more than a hundred years after Masaccio's *The Holy Trinity*. People were beginning to grow tired of the style of the first part of the Renaissance, and artists were looking for new ways to interest them. Many painters created these types of games in the 16th century, but art scholars only realized this a few decades ago. For almost 400 years, we didn't know about the anamorphoses, which are really fascinating. In this case, the artist painted what we call a memento mori (which in Latin means 'remember that you must die'). The message of the painting is: 'Whether rich or poor, beautiful or ugly, everyone dies one day.'"

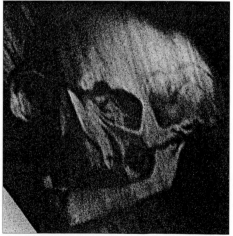

Raphaël took in his father's words slowly, realizing that there were still many puzzles to solve and things to learn before he could become a great painter, sculptor, architect, or engineer!

When Raphaël came home from school later that day, his father gave him a gift to celebrate his success. Raphaël tore open the wrapping paper and found a book and a video cassette. The book was *Anamorphoses, or the Artificial Magic of Strange Perspectives* by J. Baltrusaitis, and the cassette was *The Best Moments of the World Soccer Cup.*

After a moment's hesitation, a happy Raphaël settled comfortably on the living room sofa opposite the small television screen and dreamed of becoming a great soccer player.

Lives
of the
Artists

Raphaël

Raffaello Santi or Sanzio

"It can be said that with Raphaël painting attained perfection." (Sabba Da Castiglione, *Ricordi,* 1553). In his day, Raphaël was considered to be the greatest painter of all time. He was born in Urbino in 1483. His father, Giovanni di Santi di Pietro, was a painter. Raphaël became a *magister* (head of a painting studio) at the age of 17.

He lived in Florence from 1504 to 1508 and created many frescos and paintings. Pope Julius II entrusted him with the decoration of the Vatican Palace in Rome. The painter brought extraordinary energy to the undertaking, opening a studio and surrounding himself with numerous collaborators and students. Raphaël was also an architect and a specialist in ancient Greek and Roman art. Highly honored, he died at the age of 37 of a "high and continuous" fever.

Leonardo da Vinci

Leonardo di Ser Piero da Vinci

Born in 1452, Leonardo was the illegitimate son of a man named Ser Piero and a peasant girl named Caterina from the region of Vinci, near Florence. He was raised by his father, who settled in Florence in 1469.

Leonardo practiced painting, architecture, mathematics, geology, anatomy, botany, hydraulics, music, and ballistics. His great curiosity and tremendous knowledge made him a true Renaissance man.

Few of Leonardo's paintings have survived to our day. Only 10 works are attested to by documents and preserved in museums. Eight other paintings are mentioned in old documents but the paintings themselves have disappeared. Twelve others were commissioned from the artist, but it is unknown if they were painted by Leonardo himself. And nine other paintings are attributed to Leonardo da Vinci by specialists, but no documentation exists to confirm this supposition. Summoned to France by King François I, Leonardo participated in the organization of festivals in honor of the king. He died at the chateau d'Amboise on May 12, 1519.

Albrecht Dürer

Born in 1471 in Nürnberg, Germany, the young Albrecht apprenticed at his father's goldsmith workshop.

Dürer acquired great renown during his lifetime, especially as an engraver. He was a precocious artist, engraving a self-portrait at the age of 13. Against his father's will, the young Dürer began training at the studio of the painter Michael Wolgemut.

From 1493 to 1495, he travelled in Italy, where he discovered and copied the works of the great Renaissance painters. During a second trip to Italy in 1505, Dürer discovered the drawings of Leonardo da Vinci. By this time he enjoyed an excellent reputation as an artist and was welcomed in Venice like a prince.

In about 1512–1513, Albrecht Dürer wrote several theoretical treatises in the tradition of the great Italian Renaissance artists, including his *Treatise on Human Proportions,* which was published six months after his death in 1528.

Dürer is considered the first great German Renaissance painter.

Andrea Mantegna

Born near Vincenza in 1430 or 1431, Andrea Mantegna was greatly interested in ancient Greece and Rome, a fact that is apparent in many of his works. But his expertise in "foreshortening" is what really makes his paintings unique.

In about 1470, Mantegna worked on the decoration of the marital chamber at the chateau of Mantoue. He painted fresco scenes of court life in Mantoue, making use of the cubical room's architecture and creating a striking trompe l'oeil that would greatly influence artists later in the 16th century. He died in Mantoue in 1506.

Jan Gossart

known as Mabuse

Gossart was a Flemish painter born in Maubeuge (which earned him his nickname Mabuse) between 1478 and 1488. Nothing is known of his youth, and the first historical document we have that concerns him is a record of his enrollment in the painter's guild of Antwerp in 1503.

We also know that he went to Italy in 1508, then settled in Middelburg (the current Netherlands). He was one of the first Flemish artists to reflect the influence of Italian Renaissance artists, depicting antique architecture, nudes, and characters from ancient Greek mythology in his paintings.

He died in 1532 in the city of Breda.

Sandro Botticelli

Sandro di Mariano Filipepi

Sandro Botticelli is considered one of the greatest Renaissance painters. He worked his entire life in Florence, the city where he was born in 1445, except for a short stay in Rome from 1481 to 1482.

His characters, with their graceful postures and gently curving contours, are uniquely his own. Unlike other Renaissance painters from the early 15th century who expressed their admiration for the classical world by strictly following ancient Greek and Roman ideals about proportion in their works, Botticelli nostalgically portrayed of classical antiquity. His paintings evoke an ideal world of his own imagining.

Giorgione

Giorgio da Castelfranco

We know little about this painter, who was born in Venice in 1477 or 1478 and died at about the age of 31. Even his true name is unknown to us. He was called Zorzi during his lifetime; the name by which we know him today, Giorgione ("the great George") emerged well after his death.

In a letter dated 1510, sent to the Marquise Isabelle d'Este, Taddeo Albano wrote: "The so-called Zorzi died as much of exhaustion as of the plague."

Art historians think that Giorgione was cultured and a lover of music. His paintings are few and full of mystery.

Hans Holbein the Younger

Hans Holbein was born near Augsbourg in Germany in 1497 or 1498. His father was a painter, and it is likely he received his apprenticeship at home.

He worked in Basel, Switzerland, from 1516 to 1526, where he created portraits of rich merchants. Holbein was also known for his engravings, of which *The Macabre Dance* is the most famous.

Hans Holbein probably discovered the works of Leonardo da Vinci during a voyage to France in about 1523.

He lived in England from 1526 to 1528, settling there permanently in 1532. In London, Holbein painted numerous portraits of wealthy merchants.

He died in London in 1543.

Masaccio

Tommaso di Ser Giovanni

Considered to be one of the geniuses of the *quattrocento* ("15th century" in Italian), Tommaso di Ser Giovanni was born on December 21, 1421 (the day of Saint Thomas). His nickname, Masaccio, is a combination of *maso,* a contraction of Tommaso, and *-cio,* which is an insulting word ending in Italian. Massacio was both kind and well-liked, but he earned this mocking nickname anyway because he was a terrible dresser.

Massacio's paintings are distinguished by their precise perspectives and monumental, sculpture-like characters.

Upon the announcement of his death in 1428, Brunelleschi declared it a great loss for all.

Filippo Brunelleschi

This sculptor, architect, engineer, and artist, who was born in 1377 and died in Florence in 1446, was considered by other artists of his time to be the first modern artist. By *modern* they meant that he was the first to be interested in the art, science, and techniques of ancient Greece and Rome. He was a great engineer-architect who constructed the gigantic cupola of the Santa Maria del Fiore church in Florence, made numerous mechanical inventions, and was a master at designing irrigation systems.

Leon Battista Alberti

A poet, philologist, architect, and man of science, Alberti was very much a Renaissance man.

Born in Gênes in 1404, the young Alberti had a difficult childhood. This influenced his choice of subjects for his first writings, which deal with orphans and troubled families.

He was the author of the first modern treatises on painting and sculpture (*De Pittura* and *De Statua*). Alberti's goal was to improve the life and morality of the men of his time by drawing inspiration from the order and wealth of nature, which he studied with the help of new sciences and technology. He believed that art should imitate nature as best it can.

Alberti died in 1472.

Paolo Uccello

Paolo di Dono

Considered for centuries to be a minor painter, Uccello ("bird" in Italian) was rediscovered by surrealist artists in the early 20th century.

Paolo di Dono, called Uccello because he was known for his paintings of animals and birds in particular, was born in Florence in 1397.

The paintings attributed to Paolo Uccello show highly diverse styles and ways of thinking. Uccello considered painting to be a game and filled his works with strange scenes and extreme distortions in perspective.

He died in Florence in 1475.

Ambrogio Lorenzetti

We do not know the birth or death dates of this painter, who worked in Sienna, Italy, from 1319 to 1347.

He was one of the rare artists of this early period to paint realistic characters on a background that gives the appearance of depth.

Piero Della Francesca

Piero dei Franceschi or Piero di Benedetto or Piero dal Borgo

Piero Della Francesca, a painter and mathematician born in about 1420 in Borgo San Sepolcro, was a *quattrocento* artist who advanced the boundaries of perspective representation in painting. Piero used his knowledge of mathematics and geometry in his work. His characters and landscapes have clear geometrical volumes and occupy a precise space within his paintings.

In his treatise *De prospective pingendi*, Piero Della Francesca explained the principles of perspective representation.

The artist died in his native city on October 12, 1492.

Bernardino Pinturicchio

Bernardino Betti

Pinturicchio was born in 1454. He liked highly decorative paintings and enjoyed impressing the viewer with rich costumes or bright colors. Some of his works are filled with fabulous creatures, almost like fairy tales.

Pinturicchio died in 1513.

Domenico Ghirlandaio

Domenico Bigordi

Domenico Bigordi owes his surname Ghirlandaio (which means "maker of garlands") to his father, a goldsmith, who was famous in Florence for his marvelous hair ornaments for young girls. Ghirlandaio directed an important painting studio, and his works were often created in collaboration with his students and assistants.

The artist liked to mix scenes of daily life into his religious paintings, and his contemporary characters sometimes bear a resemblance to his clients.

Domenico Ghirlandaio died in Florence in 1494, where he was born 45 years earlier.

The Master of Flémalle

The Master, although occupying a very important place in the history of Flemish painting in the 15th century, has remained anonymous to this day. The name by which he is known today was given him long after his death by scholars who wanted to be able to discuss his work despite the fact that they did not know his real name. He was believed to be the French artist Jacques Daret, then Rogier Van der Weyden, and finally Robert Campin. The latter had a studio in Tournai, where Daret and Van der Weyden worked. Specialists attribute several works to the mysterious Master that seem to have been painted by the same person. These paintings have monumental figures that resemble colored sculptures and a very realistic perspective. The Master was the first Flemish painter to create paintings with such realistic perspective.

Art historians situate the Master of Flémalle's activity between 1410 and 1440.

Antonello da Messina

Antonello da Messina was born in Sicily in about 1430. At this time, southern Italian artistic culture was influenced by Spanish and Flemish culture, as well as by the painting of southern France. The art of Antonello combines all these influences. Nothing is known about Antonello's life between 1465 and 1472, a time when his work underwent an important transformation. His paintings completed after this time adopt the primary Renaissance principles while remaining original—their constructions are simpler than most Renaissance painting, yet they use perspective. Specialists think he may have traveled to the north of the peninsula, where Renaissance culture was blossoming. Antonello lived in Venice in 1471 and 1472, and there he created many works that would deeply influence Venetian painting.

He died in his native city in 1479.

Michelangelo

Michelangelo Buonarroti

History remembers this fabulously well-known artist by his first name. Born in Caprese, near Arezzo, in 1475, Michelangelo died in Rome in 1564.

He began his apprenticeship in the studio of Ghirlandaio in Florence in about 1488.

An audacious and prolific sculptor, architect, poet, and painter, Michelangelo Buonarroti was an artistic genius with an uncontrolled temperament.

As a painter, he is most remembered for his life's major work: the frescos of the Sistine Chapel in Rome, which, from the moment of their creation, have inspired the most extreme and diverse opinions.

"Next to Michelangelo's, any other work is vulgar scribbling" (anonymous, 16th century)

"It seems rather undesirable to me that children, women, and young girls should see these visibly immoral figures" (Ludovico Dolce, 1557).

"The greatest article of our faith was figured, or rather disfigured, by that braggart of a painter, Michelangelo" (J. J. Boissard, 1597–1602)

GLOSSARY

ambassador: a representative of the government of one country who resides in another country for diplomatic purposes

anamorphosis: a distorted optical image

Annunciation: in the Christian religion, the part of the Gospel in which the angel Gabriel announces to Mary that she will be the mother of Jesus Christ

craftsman: one who is skilled in the manual arts

depth: a front-to-back measurement taken from the point of viewing

diptych: a picture painted on two hinged tablets

distemper: a type of paint made from pigment mixed with egg yolks or whites

Flemish: of Flanders, an area encompassing present-day western Belgium and northern France

florin: a gold coin first struck in Florence, Italy, in 1252; it is no longer in use

foreshortening: a painting technique that contracts the depth of an image to make it appear as though it were projecting into space

fresco: the art of painting on freshly spread moist plaster with water based paints; any painting so executed

geometry: a branch of mathematics that deals with the measurements and relationships of points, lines, angle, surfaces, and solids

horizon: the place where the earth and sky appear to meet

intellectual: a person given to study, reflection, and speculation

Latin: a language spoken in ancient Rome and used as common language between people from different countries during the Renaissance

lute: a stringed instrument with a large, pear-shaped body

medieval: relating to or characteristic of the Middle Ages, a period of European history from about 500 to 1500

notarize: to be acknowledged by a notary public, an official who certifies that legal documents are authentic

patron: a wealthy supporter of an artist

perspective: the appearance to the eye of objects in respect to their relative distance and position

point of view: a position from which something is considered or seen

proportion: the relation of one part of a painting or scene to the other parts

Renaissance: a transitional period in European history between the Middle Ages and modern times that began in Italy in the 14th century and ended in the 17th century

Renaissance man: a person who has wide interests and is an expert in several areas

sou: a small Florentine coin of little value

theory: the abstract analysis of a set of ideas

three-dimensional: giving the illusion of having depth

triptych: a painting on three side-by-side hinged panels

vanishing point: the point at which receding parallel lines seem to meet

Photographic Credits